HOW TO QUIT
PORN

By Brett H. McKay

ISBN 978-0-9891903-4-3

Semper Virilis Publishing
PO Box 978
Jenks, OK 74037

www.sempervirilis.com

Cover by Eric Granata. Layout by Stan Perl. A Screen Four collaboration.

TABLE OF CONTENTS

INTRODUCTION

In a 2010 interview with *Playboy* magazine, musician John Mayer described his relationship with porn thusly: "It's a new synaptic pathway. You wake up in the morning, open a thumbnail page, and it leads to a Pandora's box of visuals. There have probably been days when I saw 300 vaginas before I got out of bed."

Most men in the West can identify, if not with the specific number Mayer offered, than with his general sentiment and daily routine. Viewing porn, once considered a shameful pursuit to be carried on in society's shadows, has become more than mainstream; today it's considered a nearly universal part of every man's life. Watch any modern television show (particularly sitcoms), and it is nearly assumed that the main male characters watch porn, and in many cases it's practically celebrated (see Barney in *How I Met Your Mother*). In modern novels about American life, the same is true; and even in men's magazines you'll find a variety of quips about the normalness of porn. It's become embedded into our pop culture and therefore our entertainment and our conversations.

Many men have an occasional touch of wariness about the effect their porn habit is having on their brains – even Mayer posits that it's affecting his generation's relationships later in the *Playboy* interview. But in general, viewing porn is something a lot of guys engage in without much thought, seeing it as something pretty innocuous – a normal part of life and fodder for endless jokes on internet forums.

But is porn really harmless? Should it in fact be part of a man's life, or are there potential downsides to this habit? In this book, I'll be thoroughly diving into these important questions.

What is Normal and What is Weird?

While porn is usually considered by the masses to be thoroughly healthy and decidedly normal, it is worth noting that what is "normal" in Western society doesn't necessarily hold true across cultures. In a study published in *Behavioral and Brain Sciences* (a journal published by Cambridge University), researchers found that psychologists and sociologists routinely base their conclusions on studies done with one kind of test subject: the WEIRD (those in Western, Industrialized, Rich, and Democratic societies); in fact, 96% of the subjects whose behavior has been reported in top psychological journals were drawn from only 12% of the world's population. Researchers have taken the WEIRD to be representative of populations around the globe, but this simply isn't the case. Citizens of the West are in fact more likely to be outliers when compared to the behaviors and attitudes of other cultures.

A fascinating example of this is the practice of masturbation. Like porn, masturbation is often seen as a male universal. And yet there are societies in which it is a foreign practice. Case in point: when researchers attempted to ask two Central African tribes — the Aka and the Ngandu — about their masturbation practices, the anthropologists found it difficult to explain, not because these two peoples were shy or embarrassed about the subject, but because they did not have a term for it. The researchers reported that the Aka "found it unusual and said it may happen far away in Congo, but they did not know it…We asked men, in particular, about masturbating before they were married or during the postpartum sex taboo and all indicated this did not occur[1]." The study notes that the absence of masturbation turned up among other tribes as well:

> "We asked Robert Bailey . . . about his experiences of trying to collect semen for fertility studies from Lese men in the Ituri forest of the Democratic Republic of Congo. He

> indicated it was very difficult to explain to men how to self stimulate to obtain semen samples. He said that despite explicit and lengthy instructions three of four semen specimens came to him mixed with vaginal secretions."

While masturbation and porn often go, er, hand-in-hand, the subject of this book is porn. I simply bring up the topic to demonstrate an important fact: that which we in industrialized, Western countries consider to be normal, male universals, are not always such. The claim that "everybody does it" is unfortunately often used to shut down discussions of the possible downside of certain practices before they can ever be fully examined.

Not Your Grandpappy's Porn

Of course it is true that pornography has existed for thousands of years in some form or another around the world. Neolithic cavemen likely drew naked women on the insides of caves; the ancient Greeks and Romans created art depicting graphic sex scenes; the ancient Hindus gave us the Kama Sutra; supposedly prudish Victorians still managed to create titillating erotic artwork; your grandpa lined his barracks with sexy pin-ups and had access to "stag films"; and your dad likely had a stash of *Playboy* magazines in his closet.

But the level of access and the sheer amount of porn has changed dramatically since the dawn of the digital age (in fact, it's estimated that 30% of all the data transferred on the internet is porn). In *Your Brain on Porn*, Gary Wilson argues that today's high-speed internet pornography is vastly different from the static variety of yesteryear. And, our hunter-gatherer brain simply isn't evolved for it. That mismatch — between our current porn-infused environment and what our brains are evolved for — is creating problems for many men.

The ancient, universal code of manhood rested on 3 P's: Protect, Provide, and Procreate. While the "edifice" of manhood was designed to be held up by this triad of support, in our modern age men are not often called upon to be protectors, and sometimes don't get much satisfaction from their work as providers. Consequently, the pillar of Procreation has come to bear a disproportionate amount of weight in a man's life, and has thus become twisted and contorted from the strain. The standard of procreation centered not just on having kids, but a man's sexuality as a whole, and modern men's lives are often filled to the brim with sex — or at least watching other people have sex. Men have become spectators of their own sexuality, and porn has filled their daily existence with more and more abstraction, instead of action — taking them further and further from the core of masculinity. (For more on this topic, read our series on manhood at http://aom. is/ydeQX)

Thus it is not surprising that while our culture often celebrates porn as a relatively harmless, ubiquitous pastime, fissures of discontent and concern have opened at the same time. Forums around the web are filled with thousands of men reporting a myriad of issues that have arisen from their porn use. Some have confessed that their habit has become so all-consuming that it has gotten in the way of school, work, and even relationships. Some have said that their sexual performance with their wives or girlfriends has suffered due in part to their relentless diet of porn. Some are simply tired of the way having porn on the brain has turned everything they hear — from a phrase in a pastor's sermon, to the innocent things their kids say — into a sexual innuendo. At the same time, professional urologists and therapists are beginning to report that they're seeing more and more young male patients who are heavy porn users suffer from sexual problems, like erectile dysfunction, that generally only show up later in life.

In recent years, many men have become part of the "Paleo" movement — rejiggering their diets, exercise routines, and lifestyles to align more closely with how their primitive ancestors once lived. They've discovered that sitting all day, eating processed food, and performing endless cardio was sapping their health, strength, virility, and spirit, and that creating more natural habits leveled up their lives to a new degree of vim and vigor. Is it not time that men also compared their porn consumption to that of their manly forbearers, and considered whether pulling the plug on it might aid in the journey of becoming better men?

A Note on Porn Research

Research into effects of porn use is still in all the information about porn use that I could find. However, despite the long wait, research into the effects of internet porn use is admittedly still in its infancy, and there just isn't that much out there. There are a few reasons for this. First, it's just plain hard to research the effects of porn use. Double-blind studies are impossible because if you ask a research participant to remove porn from their life, both the researcher and participant know exactly what the variable being tested is. What's more, researchers have had trouble finding men who haven't looked at internet porn to compare what their brains or lives are like compared to men who do look at porn. There's also an ethical component to the dearth of porn research. For example, a great way to study the effects of porn on the minds of teenagers would be to find a young man who hasn't looked at porn and then expose him to it. But for obvious reasons, this would not be considered ethical.

Another reason there isn't all that much research on porn is that for most of modern history, porn use was never seen as something that needed to be researched because it wasn't really seen as a problem, at least from a clinical point of view.

Finally, porn is simply a controversial issue, which makes unbiased research and analysis on it difficult. On the one hand you have moral crusaders who are gung-ho to conclusively prove that porn is absolutely terrible and should be eliminated. And on the other hand, you have "sex positive" therapists, sexologists, and yes, porn producers who think porn use is part of a sexually healthy lifestyle and consequently downplay evidence of porn's detriments while emphasizing its benefits.

All this is to say that sussing out solid, unbiased porn-related research is difficult. However, that's beginning to change. As more and more men on internet forums self-report having problems with internet porn, and as the number of doctors and therapists report seeing patients who are having trouble with porn, researchers are starting to give porn use, particularly the online variety, a serious look.

Until more research is done on the effect of viewing internet porn on the body and mind, we're left with using correlational and anecdotal evidence about its effects. While not as strong as causal studies, and deserving of greater scrutiny, it would be foolhardy to dismiss this evidence that we do have altogether. Much of the research and analysis about porn use is being done by men who have experienced problems with it firsthand. They've come together on forums around the web (like *Your Brain on Porn*) to take part in a giant n=1 experiment by seeing what happens when they eliminate porn from their lives and reporting the results. It's admittedly not the most scientifically rigorous form of experimentation, but their shared experiences have proven useful to other men and have spurred actual scientists to put internet porn under the microscope even more.

A Note on My Own Biases

I would be remiss if I did not at the outset disclose my own biases as to the subject of porn. To put all my cards on the table, I personally think porn is wrong and immoral. I'm a religious guy, so sexual chastity, on a variety of levels, is a standard I subscribe to. Other than discovering some nudie mags in the woods as a boy, and occasionally inadvertently stumbling on pornography on the web (it's hard not to when your job is on the internet), I'm not a porn user and never have been.

In some people's eyes, this likely renders me incapable of putting out objective material about porn. While that's true, no one is objective, even professional scientists. And I personally think I am pretty adept at examining a subject apart from my own beliefs, approaching it as a neutral observer would, and trying to see if there are any compelling, non-religious reasons to adopt certain behaviors. To that end, my research has been all over the spectrum, and I intentionally read both pro-, and anti-porn materials with an open mind. In fact, at one point in my research, I came to think that while porn wasn't for me because of my personal beliefs, it really wasn't a big deal for other men, and did not have significantly deleterious effects. But then, after reading more materials on the subject, I ultimately came to feel that the argument against using porn was in fact the strongest, regardless of a person's religious beliefs.

Finally, despite my faith, I'm not a fan of the firebrand anti-porn scare messages put out there by many of the religious ilk. I can't help but roll my eyes when people call porn a "pandemic" or "plague." From my observations, I just don't think that sort of rhetoric is all that helpful and in fact can actually backfire — making the allure of porn even more enticing and the specter of quitting even more difficult for men who are using it (I'll explain why later in the book).

Bottom line: I intend to present information on the possible negative effects of porn use in the most even-handed, non-polemical way possible, and allow readers to draw their own conclusions about whether viewing porn is a habit they want to keep or not.

Where We're Going

In this book, I will be offering an in-depth look at what the growing research suggests about internet porn's effect on the brain. If you've been struggling to stop using porn (for whatever reason), you'll learn why it's such a hard thing to kick (but how it's still possible). Here's what is on deck:

Chapter 1

Porn, dopamine, and your brain; you'll learn the important role that dopamine plays in your craving for porn.

Chapter 2

How internet porn creates a powerful "super-stimulus" that can rewire your brain's reward circuitry, making you feel like you're addicted and can't stop. We'll also look at how over-consumption of internet porn can cause sexual problems like erectile dysfunction and delayed ejaculation, even in young, healthy men, along with emotional and social problems like depression, social anxiety, and decrease in willpower. By understanding the neuroscience of internet porn, you'll be in a better position to stop using it.

Chapter 3

We'll conclude with some tips from the fields of cognitive and behavioral psychology that can help you quit porn for good.

CHAPTER 1

Men and Porn: Why is the Pull of Porn so Strong?

The first step in understanding the effects of porn on your brain is to understand the relationship between your noodle and dopamine, and how this interplay makes the pull of porn so strong. I truly feel that understanding this dynamic is the crucial foundation to making a decision about what role you want porn to play in your life, and also to ultimately quitting this habit.

Dopamine and Your Brain

Our brains are composed of billions of cells called neurons that send messages to each other through an electrical-chemical process. Without getting too technical about how this works, the important thing to understand for this discussion is that the neuron delivering the message releases a chemical called a neurotransmitter into the synapse — the space between the neurons — and over to a receiving neuron. The receiving neuron catches the neurotransmitter with its receptors and then generates electricity so it can communicate to another neuron. This process repeats itself a bajillion (that's a scientific term) times a day.

Different neurotransmitters communicate different things. What they all have in common is that their primary purpose isn't to make you "happy" or fulfilled, but to ensure that your carcass survives so that you can pass on your genes.

An integral part of our brain's system for increasing our chances of survival and reproduction is creating the strong desire and drive to do or seek out those things that will help us fulfill those aims. We have to want to eat, we have to want to seek shelter, and we have to want to have sex. The neurotransmitter that gives us our drive to fulfill these impulses is dopamine.

Dopamine is released whenever we encounter rewards, or "natural reinforcers," that help us survive. Things like food, sex, novelty (new things may lead to new survival-boosting benefits), and friendship (you're more likely to survive in a group) sit at the top of the natural reinforcer hierarchy. Once we encounter one of these potent rewards/reinforcers, a neural pathway is created (more on neural pathways below). Dopamine keys in on the reward system in our brain, and drives us to repeat the same behaviors that helped us attain those rewards previously.

The more something helps with our survival and reproduction, the bigger the "squirt" of dopamine our neurons experience, and the stronger the drive to repeat the behavior. For example, different types of food release different levels of dopamine. Because our hunter-gatherer ancestors lived in feast and famine mode, it made evolutionary sense to load up on as many calories as possible while the getting was good. Foods high in fat and sugar provided the most energy benefits, so our ancestors' brains evolved to release a lot of dopamine when they encountered high fat and high sugar foods. Our brains continue to do the same thing in the modern word, which explains why when given the choice between a Five Guys burger and a dry salad, our gut instinct is to go with the burger and shake. Dopamine drives us towards sweet, carby, and high fat foods.

Sexual stimulation and orgasm give our brain's reward system the biggest *natural* shot of dopamine of all. Which makes sense. From an evolutionary perspective, the entire measure of our creation is to reproduce and pass on our genes. So seeking for and wanting sex should be our primary evolutionary drive. That big dopamine shot that results from orgasm then goes on to wire our brain's reward system to repeat whatever behavior we did to get sex so we can continue to get sex in the future.

ISN'T TESTOSTERONE RESPONSIBLE FOR MY SEX DRIVE?

Contrary to popular belief and cheesy internet ads, it isn't testosterone that plays a central role in a man's sexual libido and ability to get an erection, it's dopamine[1]. Testosterone plays more of a supportive role in our sex drive by stimulating the brain to produce more dopamine. So while low T can result in low libido, it's because there isn't enough T to stimulate sufficient dopamine for a healthy sex drive. It is therefore possible for a man to have high total and free testosterone levels, but low dopamine (or blunted dopamine sensitivity – more on that later), and thus a low or absent sex drive. Testosterone's dopamine-stimulating abilities also explain why testosterone replacement therapy companies advertise that increasing your T can give you more energy and drive to do other stuff in life. It's not the T itself, but rather the dopamine that T triggers in the brain that gives you that boost. The more you know.

The release of dopamine starts amping up your sex drive when you see someone attractive. This increase will motivate you to do whatever your culture says you need to do to woo that person and eventually get them into bed. If you're the old-fashioned type, that process can take a while. If you're a Don Juan and the gal is open to casual sex, maybe a few hours is all you'll need. Whatever the timetable, dopamine levels and hence sex drive will continue to increase as you move towards consummating your desire. The powerful urge to copulate created by spiking levels of dopamine as you get closer and closer to actually having sex partly explains those moments when people say, "I don't know what happened. One moment we were on the couch watching *Louie* and the next minute we were making the beast with two backs."

Once we achieve whatever reward dopamine was driving us towards, the levels of this neurotransmitter drop off. With sex, dopamine levels peak right around the moment of orgasm (to help wire our brains to seek out sex again in the future), but then decrease afterwards because we've accomplished our biological imperative to spread our seed. (Your brain doesn't know if your seed never made it past the end of your condom. As far as your neurons are concerned, it's "mission accomplished.") The post-coitus drop in dopamine partly explains the male "refractory period" after sex. (In case you didn't know, after a man orgasms, it's physiologically impossible for him to have another orgasm for a period of time. Could be minutes, could be days. Depends on the guy.) When we orgasm, a hormone called prolactin is released which represses dopamine. No dopamine, no sex drive, no boner.

Porn, Novelty, and the Coolidge Effect

Remember when I mentioned above that one of our evolved natural reinforcers is novelty? Our brains are hardwired to seek out novelty because new things can provide survival and reproductive advantages. Whenever we encounter anything new — a new email, a new gadget, a new food — we get a shot of dopamine, which makes us want to look for more new things. We've all got an irrepressible treasure hunter streak in us. Thanks to a process called habituation, the familiar just doesn't provide the same kind of dopamine hit as the novel. Habituation explains why the new car that we were so motivated to get for months and months doesn't excite us nearly as much after just a few weeks of driving it around town.

We also get that shot of dopamine whenever we encounter a new attractive woman other than our current partner. Our brains are hardwired to seek out as many different (novel) sexual partners as possible. Again, from a reproductive perspective it makes sense that being exposed to a variety of attractive sex partners would jack up dopamine in our sexual reward circuitry, particularly in men. For males, the goal is to reproduce with as many different females as possible to create as many progeny as possible, with as much genetic variation as possible to increase our possible blood lines.

This drive for multiple new sex partners even when you already have an available and willing one is often called the "Coolidge Effect" after a conversation the president supposedly had with his wife:

> The President and Mrs. Coolidge were being shown [separately] around an experimental government farm. When [Mrs. Coolidge] came to the chicken yard she noticed that a rooster was mating very frequently. She asked the attendant how often that happened and was told, "Dozens of times each day." Mrs. Coolidge said, "Tell that to the President when he comes by." Upon being told, President asked, "Same hen every time?" The reply was, "Oh, no, Mr. President, a different hen every time." To which the president replied, "Tell that to Mrs. Coolidge."

To understand the power the Coolidge Effect has in increasing dopamine levels let's take a look at two experiments.

In the first, a lucky male rat was placed in a cage with four or five female rats. He immediately had sex with all of them until exhaustion. Panting and rolled over in a sexual stupor, the male rat was nudged and licked by the female rats to keep going, but he didn't respond. The tuckered-out rodent was no longer interested in doing the deed. But as soon as the researchers put a new female rat in the cage, old Mr. I'm Too Tired became alert and sarged over to have sex with the new female, while ignoring his old harem. This rat's ability to have sex with a new female despite having been previously sexually satiated all came down to dopamine. The first crew no longer gave him those potent dopamine shots because, well, they were now boring. Been there, done that. But the new female caused an uptick in dopamine due to novelty and bam! the male rat's sex drive was back[2]. The Coolidge Effect explains why people are tempted to cheat, even with someone significantly less attractive that their long-term partner; the pull of novelty, any novelty, can be quite strong.

A similar experiment was done to show the Coolidge Effect in humans. Instead of putting a lone man in a room with four or five different women to have sex with (there likely would have been plenty of volunteers, but the ethicality would have been questionable), researchers showed test subjects an erotic film while their penises were attached to monitors to measure arousal. After 18 viewings of the same film, arousal had decreased dramatically. These guys had gotten used to seeing the same woman having sex with the same dude, so dopamine levels dropped. But on the 19th and 20th viewings, researchers showed a new clip and atten-hut! arousal skyrocketed once again. Sexual novelty increased dopamine levels, which increased sexual arousal[3].

How Online Porn Has Changed Your Brain

Alright. So what does all of the above have to do with internet porn?

Well, dopamine plays a central role in why you want to look at porn. Understand how dopamine works, and you understand why you are attracted to porn.

Porn is a substitute for actual sex, but your brain doesn't know that. It reacts to a picture of a naked woman or a video of people having sex the same way it does a real life naked woman or you actually having sex. When encountering sexual images, your brain is going to ramp up dopamine levels, driving you to orgasm — whether that climax is fostered with another human being or is self-induced[4].

Dopamine also explains why certain types of porn are more compelling than others, and how in extreme cases men prefer porn to actual sex.

A still picture of a naked woman will jack up dopamine levels the first time you see it, but after a while that same picture just won't do it for you any more. Your brain has become *habituated* to that stimulus. In order to be aroused again, you'd need to increase dopamine levels by injecting more novelty into your sexual fantasies with a new picture of a different naked woman.

But as time goes on, simply looking at any picture of a naked woman won't get you aroused. You need something more. Well, you get a bigger shot of dopamine whenever you watch others have sex in a porn video because the live action activates your mirror neurons, making you feel like you're the one having sex. The stronger the stimulation, the bigger the shot of dopamine to the reward system, and hence the greater desire you have to watch that porn video.

But as the study above showed, after repeated viewings, even an erotic film can become like watching a boring documentary. It just won't offer the same kind of dopamine hit you got the first time you watched it, and will eventually fail to arouse you. Again, this is due to habituation. To become sexually aroused again, you need to increase dopamine levels by watching something new, be it a video with a new woman or a video with some new sex practice you've never seen before. Add the novelty, increase the dopamine, and sexual arousal returns.

You're probably seeing a common theme here: novelty. Porn offers the sexual novelty that dopamine has hardwired you to seek. The more you successfully find new sexual experiences, the more dopamine you get, which reinforces the desire to look for even more sexual novelty. Porn's easy access to new "experiences" is part of what makes it so alluring.

Now before the internet, this wasn't much of a problem. Once a man in the pre-internet porn years got habituated to his "girly" magazine, he had to trek over to the adult bookshop or the convenience store in the seedy part of town to get a new one. If he wanted to watch a pornographic film, he'd have to go to a XXX theatre or maybe a porno booth in that bookstore where he got his mags. Whether getting magazines or seeing films, it was a lot of rigmarole to get porn, plus there was the risk of getting caught and experiencing social shame. So, many men just didn't bother. Even when he could have the magazines or videos delivered to his home, that happened maybe once or twice a month. If he had kids, he had to find a place to stash his porn and then find time when his family wasn't around so he could exhume his collection and view it in privacy. Again, a lot of rigmarole.

So while porn offered some sexual novelty back in the day, there were barriers put in place due to technology (or the lack thereof) and social mores that made access to new and novel porn difficult and time-consuming. Because the dopamine hits from the new and novel didn't come easy, getting hooked on porn was difficult and most men didn't experience the many problems that modern porn users report.

Fast-forward to today. Thanks to the internet, you now have an infinite variety of porn on tap 24/7. Dopamine spikes due to sexual novelty have never been easier to achieve. No more trudging to the adult bookstore, no more going to great lengths to hide your porn. Just bring it up on your laptop or mobile device in the privacy of your home or at the bathroom at work. You can have multiple tabs open in your browser for different porn sites featuring a whole host of different virtual sex partners. As Gary Wilson notes in *Your Brain on Porn*, in "ten minutes, you can 'experience' more novel sex partners than your hunter-gatherer ancestors experienced in a lifetime."

Internet porn doesn't just provide access to novel sex "partners," but to novel sexual experiences as well. You're not just limited to watching a couple have sex missionary style, but can watch a wide variety of sexual acts. Just as novel sex partners will jack up dopamine levels, so will observing different sex acts. And as we'll discuss in the next chapter, dopamine levels also spike when we encounter things that shock us or gross us out. The more intense the emotional experience we have when we encounter porn, the more dopamine is released into our brain's reward system. Which is why you may find yourself searching for kinkier and kinkier porn even though part of you finds it repulsive. All of this novelty is just a click away. As you experience more and more dopamine shots to your reward system with new types of porn, connections in your brain's reward circuitry strengthen, increasing your drive to seek even more sexual novelty. On and on the cycle goes.

Neuroplasticity or, Why You Have the Urge to Look at Porn Whenever You Get Bored or Open Up Your Web Browser

So dopamine is what drives you to want to look at porn. And thanks to the internet, you have access to an unlimited variety of sexual "experiences" that when viewed, send out shot after shot of dopamine in your brain, which drives you to search for more and more porn.

At the same time, without you even knowing it, those dopamine shots are also strengthening neural connections that are responsible for the behavior that keeps those neuro-transmitter hits coming.

Porn is literally rewiring your brain.

You've probably heard the phrase "neurons that fire together, wire together." It aptly describes the way we learn things. Everything you know — how to walk, how to throw a football, who won the World Series in 1989 — is made up of connected neurons firing in sync with one another. The stronger the connection, the less you have to think about doing or remembering the thing you're trying to recall. You don't have to think about walking, for instance, because the neurons involved in walking have a strong connection that began being formed as toddler. However, trying to remember information for a history test that you just crammed for the previous night might be more difficult because the neurons involved in that memory haven't fired enough together to create a strong connection.

Neurons firing and wiring together is also how our habits are formed. When you receive a shot of dopamine after receiving some reward, be it food or sex or novelty, your brain is strengthening the neurons that fired and wired together to achieve the reward so that you will repeat the process and can get it again in the future[5]. This rewiring involves connecting the cues and behavior that led to a respective reward.

This cue-behavior-reward connection is what author Charles Duhigg calls "The Habit Loop," and understanding it can go a long way in helping you understand and break your porn habit.

Habit researchers have shown that almost all cues (the thing that reminds or triggers your brain to seek a reward through a certain behavior) fall into one of five categories:

- Location
- Time
- Emotional State
- Other People

• Immediately-preceding Action

Again, your brain is paying attention to cues that are connected with the reward. Once it recognizes the cue, dopamine is released to get you craving and wanting to do whatever it takes to get the reward. Think Pavlov's dogs here. At the beginning of that experiment, it was just food that got the dogs salivating. But then they were introduced to the cue of a metronome, and after a while just that sound would get them salivating for their reward.

With porn, the associated cue could be sitting down at your computer late at night when everyone else is asleep. If you're John Mayer, the cue would be being in bed when you first get up in the morning. For many guys, being in bed right before they go to sleep is a cue. Coming across a porn image by accident while surfing Tumblr could be a cue to start looking for more porn. Heck, just visiting Tumblr might be a cue to start looking for more porn.

Cues don't even have to be external. The most common porn surfing cues are emotional states. Many men find themselves surfing for porn when they're depressed or bored or even distracted. For them, the pleasure of porn offers relief from these unpleasant emotions.

Once the cue triggers the dopamine production that ramps up your motivation to view porn, a behavioral routine is automatically set in motion. A routine is a behavior or set of behaviors that get you to the reward of orgasm. So let's say your cue to look for porn is when you're at your computer late at night after everyone has gone to bed. Once that happens, without even really thinking about it, you open up your web browser (in incognito mode, of course) and go right to PornHub to commence a session of porn browsing and masturbating. The cue-behavior/routine-reward circuit is complete. Your brain releases a huge shot of dopamine right around orgasm, reinforcing the neural connections associated with the cue, routine, and reward so that next time you have the same cue (at your computer late at night), you'll get that itch to start your routine to get more porn. Repeat this circuit over a period of a few days or weeks, and you've got yourself a strong neural connection that leads to you checking out porn without even really thinking about it. That's how porn can become a strong habit or even an addiction (we'll talk more about the habit vs. addiction distinction in the next chapter).

Recap

Let's review what we've covered in this chapter.

The reason porn is so alluring is because of dopamine. Dopamine is what makes us crave or seek out evolutionarily advantageous rewards. Sex is the strongest natural reinforcer of behavior and releases the most amount of dopamine in our brain when we successfully orgasm. Our brain doesn't differentiate between porn-induced sex fantasies and actual sex, so we get the same big hit of dopamine, and the same incredibly strong drive to orgasm, with porn as we do with real life sex. Basically, when you look at porn, your brain thinks you're a heroic tribesman out on the savanna, and is shouting "Atta boy! Spread that seed! Spread that seed!" when in reality you're hunched over your laptop, the light of the screen illuminating your dead-eyed gaze, as you clench a wad of tissues.

The more habituated we get to a stimulus, the less dopamine our brains release in conjunction with it. Getting the same hit as before necessitates seeking out sexual novelty, and high-speed internet porn provides this in spades. This easy access to a wide variety of new sexual scenes and practices makes internet porn all the more alluring and desirable thanks to the dopamine hits your brain gets every time you click over to a new porn clip or picture.

Not only does dopamine create the craving to surf for porn, it's also strengthening the neural connections in your reward circuitry that are responsible for the behaviors that lead to you actually looking at and masturbating to porn. Your brain comes to associate certain environmental or internal cues with the reward of orgasm so that whenever you encounter these cues, a behavioral routine is initiated that leads you to your favorite porn site. Your brain releases more dopamine in response to successfully getting porn, and orgasming from it, which strengthens this neural cue-routine-reward circuit, making porn surfing a habit that's extremely difficult to shake.

And there you have the brain science of why internet porn is so incredibly alluring and habit-forming.

But, the question remains...should you even care? Why not just give the old brain what it craves and not worry about it? To the possible negative effects of this course, is where we will turn in chapter 2.

CHAPTER 2

The Possible Pitfalls of Porn

In recent years, more and more young men — religious and not — are reporting that they feel outright addicted to internet pornography. Thousands and thousands are filling online porn recovery forums to discuss their struggles, opening up to total strangers rather than their friends and family. It has consumed their lives and gets in the way of school, work, and relationships. Time that could be spent on their goals is instead spent hunched over a glowing screen with a box of Kleenex and lotion. Some men report that they prefer masturbating to porn to having actual sex with an honest to goodness real life woman. In fact, more and more healthy young men in their early 20s are visiting their doctors asking for Viagra because they no longer can get or maintain an erection with their sexual partner[1]. Many of these young men happen to be heavy internet porn users.

What's more, they report finding themselves turned on by increasingly disturbing sexual material, like gang rape scenes, as their porn use increases. They want to stop because, on a gut level, the material repulses them, but they feel like they have to watch the stuff because it's the only way they can become sexually aroused.

What's going on here?

We've already established that internet porn is extremely alluring and habit forming thanks to how easy it is to access an unlimited variety of sensory intensive videos. But because of the nature of internet porn, it can cause a whole host of problems beyond an intense craving to watch it after everyone has gone to bed.

In the world of evolutionary biology and human psychology it has been proven that animals and humans will often prefer exaggerated versions of a reward stimulus over one they'd encounter normally in nature, and — here's the kicker — even if the attraction to the exaggerated version of the stimulus is evolutionarily and reproductively harmful. This is called a *supernormal stimulus.*

We see multiple examples of this in the animal kingdom: Birds will sit and take care of fake eggs that resemble those of their own species, but are larger and have more exaggerated markings and a richer hue. Territorial male stickleback fish will attack wooden floats painted red on the bottom if the wooden floats are painted a more intense shade of red than what's found on their actual, natural enemies. Male jewel beetles will prefer to copulate with a certain type of beer bottle cap rather than actual female jewel beetles because the cap looks like an exaggerated version of their natural copulation partners.

We see supernormal stimuli influence human beings as well. Junk food is a supernormal stimulus of the salty, fatty, and sugary foods that our brains are naturally evolved to crave. In fact, as the book *Salt Sugar Fat* highlights, food companies spend millions of dollars engineering food with the perfect combination of these ingredients. These supernormal foods are designed to precisely activate our "bliss point" — registering as incredibly tasty while simultaneously compelling us to eat more. Think of the sensation of eating a Dorito, and the feel of that salt, sugar, and fat on your tongue; once one is down the hatch, you immediately want another chip.

In the area of sex and porn, male humans (generally) prefer exaggerated versions of female sex traits — big boobs, smaller waists, big hips. Make-up is designed and applied to accentuate and exaggerate features on the female face that males find attractive like the lips and eyes.

The likely reason supernormal stimuli are so much more alluring than ho-hum natural simulations is due to — you guessed it — our old friend dopamine. More dopamine is released when we encounter a supernormal stimulus than with the rewards found in nature.

Porn is the ultimate supernormal stimulus of our naturally-evolved desire for sex. For starters, porn often features exaggerated versions of female and male bodies doing exaggerated versions of sex, e.g., women with cantaloupe-sized tatas moaning loudly during marathon sex sessions with not just one but two or more men sporting giant penises artificially made erect by the injection of Caverject. If that's not a supernormal stimulus, I don't know what is.

Add in the visual intensity that video porn offers over static images or sex fantasies produced in the mind, and the unlimited variety of these films that are just a click away, and you've got a recipe for a super-super-normal stimulus. Compared to normal women and normal sex, internet porn likely provides stronger hits of dopamine, making it much more desirable.

Just as our physical bodies were not evolved for a diet consisting of Doritos and Twinkies, our brains were not evolved for the massive dopamine hits that today's internet porn provides. To protect itself from the unnatural uptick in dopamine, the brain reduces the number of dopamine receptors in the neurons involved with sexual reward. And this is where we run into problems with the over-consumption of porn. Let's take a more in-depth look at them.

The Potential Cognitive and Emotional Problems of Habitual Porn Use

THE NEED TO FIND JUST THE RIGHT
STIMULUS TO GET AROUSED.

When there are fewer dopamine receptors on deck, as mentioned above, the porn user can't feel the full force of the neurotransmitter's effect. The receptors become *desensitized*. Thus to get the same buzz and reward, the consumer has to go looking for some new porn that provides the same level of arousal as before. So a user moves from sex scenes on cable TV shows, to amateur hardcore porn sites on the web. But after a while that doesn't do it any more, so he begins the search again. The task of looking for just the right scene to get the blood flowing can begin to take longer and longer, as the user clicks through hundreds of sites and files to find the situation he thinks will do the trick. It's what Mayer called in his aforementioned interview with *Playboy*, "the shot hunt":

> "Internet pornography has absolutely changed my generation's expectations. How could you be constantly synthesizing an orgasm based on dozens of shots? You're looking for the one photo out of 100 you swear is going to be the one you finish to, and you still don't finish. Twenty seconds ago you thought that photo was the hottest thing you ever saw, but you throw it back and continue your shot hunt and continue to make yourself late for work."

The daily "shot hunt" is not only time-consuming, but can cause problems when you're trying to orgasm in real life, and the only "shot" you've got to work with is the woman beneath you.

TURNING TO INCREASINGLY KINKIER PORN.

For many men, even finding the "perfect" scene of "normal" porn stops doing it for them. Their dopamine receptors are so blunted, they need something a lot more hardcore to get going, and they soon discover that porn that's incredibly shocking, and in many cases even illegal (rape, bestiality, child pornography) makes them feel both guilty and aroused. With some hesitation, and a bit of a pit in their stomach, but with the drive for the return of their old dopamine levels spurring them on, they click on stuff that goes well beyond a normal sexual experience. And if you think that these are "extreme" examples, think again: up to 88% of all the scenes in porn videos involve some type of aggression, be it hitting, gagging, slapping, verbal abuse, etc[2].; a shocking 1/3 of internet porn searches have the word "teen" and *it's the most searched for type of porn* according to PornHub's statisticians; and sadly, the Internet Watch Foundation reports that child pornography is one of the internet's fastest growing "businesses," with viewership growing over 1,000 percent in the last ten years.

Why is this? Well, dopamine production fires up when we experience intense emotions, and that includes shock, anxiety, and guilt. Add those dopamine-producing emotions to an already dopamine-stimulating input like sex, and you have a recipe for being aroused by kinkier and kinkier porn. As men become *desensitized* to one type of porn, they must keep searching for more and more exaggerated and shocking types of sexual imagery to get the same kind of buzz as they did before.

ERECTILE DYSFUNCTION AND OTHER PERFORMANCE ISSUES.

As we mentioned in the previous chapter, dopamine plays a big role in our sex drive, libido, and ability to get and maintain an erection. Reduce dopamine or blunt the reception of it, and bamo, no more boners. And that's exactly what's happening to more and more young men who are over-consuming internet pornography. The constant flood of dopamine eventually reduces the brain's receptors for this neurotransmitter, which in turn blunts sexual arousal when they actually want to have sex with a human being.

Because these young men have conditioned themselves to be aroused by a super-stimulus version of sex, normal sex (the kind we're evolved for) just isn't arousing anymore[3]. Many men report having to watch porn before and/or while they have sex with their significant other, just so they can get an erection. If porn's not available while they have sex, they have to replay porn images in their head in order to maintain their erection. What's more, many men report on forums and to their doctors that they can no longer orgasm while having real sex. They can hump and pump for hours and not ejaculate. While the idea that you can last that long sounds good in theory, the inability to achieve orgasm with your partner may create significant issues in your relationship (not to mention her physical discomfort). Orgasm in both men and women releases large amounts of powerful hormones like oxytocin and prolactin that help bond a couple together. Sex that frequently and unintentionally ends without orgasm will almost certainly create frustration and distance between partners.

Further, a woman who can't arouse or pleasure her man is likely to feel that she's no longer attractive or desirable to him, which can be devastating to her sense of self-worth. And she's actually right to feel insecure: studies show that people who look at porn find their partners less attractive. But the potential relationship problems don't end there....

RELATIONSHIP TENSION CAUSED BY A
MISMATCH OF EXPECTATIONS.

Studies on the effect of men's porn use on the intimacy and sexual satisfaction of their relationships have found it to be almost uniformly negative. This negative effect arises on several fronts:

First, a guy's penchant for porn can make his partner feel less attractive — like she can't measure up to the supernormal babes in her boyfriend's favorite videos. When college women were surveyed, those who felt their boyfriend's use of porn was problematic reported lower self-esteem, relationship quality, and sexual satisfaction[4].

Second, the APA reports that men's porn use is "associated with lower sexual quality for both men and their partners" as well as "lower levels of sexual intimacy in their real-life relationships." This is especially true when someone uses porn at a high rate, as this tends to lead to emotional withdrawal and "increased secrecy, less intimacy and also more depression." Psychologists are not sure if high porn use causes these negative effects, or is correlated with them; does porn use make the relationship rocky, or is the relationship rocky already, leading the man to turn to porn for sexual satisfaction? They argue that it is likely both, and that the factors end up feeding each other: "If a couple goes through a dry spell, the man may watch more porn to fill the void. Some women may feel threatened or confused by that response. They often report feeling less attractive, like they could never measure up to the X-rated actresses. The result: even less sex, even more porn and a relationship that continues to falter[5]."

Another way porn can get in the way of healthy and strong relationships is that it may be teaching you unrealistic sexual practices that you or your partner aren't comfortable with. One of the most powerful ways we learn how to do things is by watching others. This is thanks to mirror neurons. If your sexual education has come largely from viewing hardcore internet pornography, you're probably, consciously or not, learning what you think "normal" sex should be like from it.

In porn, women scream in ecstasy after a guy ejaculates on her face. That turns you on and the woman in the video seemed to like it so you figure your sexual partner would like it too. So you give it a go only to find your mate is stunned or even repulsed by the act. What is often forgotten is that sex in porn is choreographed to turn on a third-party viewer, not for the people actually taking part in the sex. Replicating sex scenes you see in porn is the equivalent of replicating martial arts moves you saw in a kung fu movie in an actual street fight. It doesn't translate well.

In a recent study amongst British teens, both boys and girls have reported feeling pressured into engaging in anal sex even when they didn't enjoy it all that much. Several reasons were given, including avoiding the risk of pregnancy, but the young adults also reported that they felt pressured to do so because that's what they've seen in porn[6]. This isn't to say that it isn't possible for men or women to enjoy anal sex — plenty do — but this study bolsters the idea that pornography may be unconsciously conditioning you to engage in sexual practices that you and your partner don't actually want to try, but feel you "should" engage in.

Now, it is certainly true that there are absolutely women out there who are up for all sorts of kinky things. I'm not saying this isn't the case. What I am saying is that if a guy has been a heavy porn user, and his partner hasn't been, he may try to get her to do things she isn't comfortable with. And if both parties have watched a good amount of porn, they may try to create a sex life based on what they have learned is "normal," even if they're not actually enjoying it. *Man initiates awkward attempts at strange positions; woman screams and moans loudly, just like she's seen the porn stars do.* Both partners can feel like they're playing inauthentic roles, and neither feels like they're keeping it real.

If you want to try out new sexual practices with your partner, look through a book together on the subject — one with boring, static diagrams. And together decide what you'd like to give a whirl. That way, you're both on the same page, and you don't have a slickly-produced video to compare your own likely awkward and humorously executed results with.

DEPRESSION, LOSS OF IMPULSE CONTROL, AND SOCIAL ANXIETY.

Many men who use porn heavily report several behavioral and emotional problems. Depression, impulse control, and social anxiety are some of the top ones. Now it could be the case (and often is) that the reason men who use porn heavily have these issues isn't because they consume porn, but rather that they heavily consume porn because they have these issues. Porn, like drugs or alcohol, is often a way to self-medicate and to make yourself feel better. For these men, treating the underlying issue — be it depression or social anxiety — can help them stop using porn as much.

However, it is also possible that porn use can cause these problems, and that they can be traced to structural and chemical changes in the brain that can accompany heavy porn use. Recent research has shown that the dopamine desensitization that comes with prolonged exposure to an excess of dopamine can cause depression[7]. Which makes sense. One symptom of depression is the lack of motivation to do things that once brought you joy. Dopamine is the neurotransmitter of motivation, so if your brain is desensitized to it, motivation decreases, and you get into a funk. Many men on porn recovery forums have reported that once they eliminated porn from their lives, symptoms of depression alleviated as well.

Many men in those forums also report having social anxiety or extreme shyness, which has gotten in the way of advancing their careers and in forming nurturing romantic relationships. Studies indicate that reduced dopamine receptor sensitivity might be partly to blame for this issue[8]. Here again, men who have self-reported have found that eliminating porn from their lives reduced or eliminated that anxiety. By eliminating the source of overweening dopamine production, their synapses were able to "heal" by getting dopamine receptors back to normal.

Finally, habitual porn use may cause a weakening of brain activity in your prefrontal cortex (PFC) called hypofrontality. The PFC is the disciplined, executive part of your brain that helps you act in a way that aligns with your goals. It's what helps you plan for the future, stops you from eating that Twinkie when you're trying to go Paleo, and keeps you from surfing away from a long article on the web in order to check Reddit. While there are several factors that lead to hypofrontality, research suggests that reduced dopamine receptors in the PFC is part of what weakens your executive functioning, leading to a reduction in willpower and impulse control[9]. This is yet another reason why men who look at porn, but want to stop, have a hard time doing so — their ability to say no to their primal drives has been weakened by the very thing they're trying to quit.

Yet again, men who have been able to eliminate porn from their lives report seeing an increase in willpower and impulse control that impacts not just their ability to stay away from porn but all areas of their lives. They find they procrastinate less and have an easier time sticking with goals they've set for themselves.

Is Porn Use an Addiction?

What about when porn use turns into a full-blown addiction? Is that another one of its pitfalls? Can it even truly become an addiction or is it just a habit?

Suffice it to say, these questions are the subject of much heated debate.

Currently the DSM-5, the Bible of psychiatric diagnosis (which, just like the actual Bible, is super controversial) does not consider behaviors like porn use, eating, or gambling, to be addictions. Only dependence on *substances*, like drugs, alcohol, and nicotine, are "officially" considered addictions. The list includes things like strong cravings for the substance, the creation of professional and relationship problems, needing more and more of the substance to get the same high as before, difficulty quitting, and withdrawal symptoms when doing so.

Looking over that list, one can easily see how certain behaviors outside drug and alcohol use would seem to qualify as an addiction. Millions of people have reported behaviors like compulsive gambling, shopping, and web surfing as meeting several of the criteria.

So, while the DSM-5 still does not currently consider behaviors to technically be addictions, a case could be made for labeling compulsive porn viewing as such. Different studies have both supported and contradicted the idea of porn being addictive. Ultimately, drawing the line between habit and addiction is always going to be subjective, no matter what scientific research and opinions are brought to bear on the question.

Given the inherent squigginess of the habit vs. addiction spectrum, I personally strongly believe that it's better to frame it as the former. This is not at all to downplay the severity of compulsive porn use, nor to deny its extremely strong pull. Rather, it's because I think porn is such a problem, that I believe calling it a habit is the best way to go. Let me explain why.

Labeling impulsive behaviors as addictions may hinder an individual from feeling capable of conquering an undesirable behavior. "Addiction" is a very loaded — even scary — word. When we tell ourselves we have an addiction, we're implying that we've lost control of ourselves, that our ability to make our own choices is impaired, and that it may even be impossible to change course. Something else is in the driver's seat, so to speak.

Thus, calling an undesirable behavior an addiction has the tendency to shift us from an internal locus of control to an external one. That is, you believe an external force is in control of your life rather than you. Research has shown that those with an internal locus exhibit greater control over their behavior and deal with challenges and stress better. Those with an external locus of control, on the other hand, feel like they're a victim of powers outside themselves, which leads to stress, anxiety, and depression. The desire to soothe these hopeless feelings will then often lead right back to porn. And on the cycle will go.

Religious Men and Porn Addiction

Another problem with framing habits as addictions is that there's a tendency to label any undesirable behavior as such, even though the pattern of behavior doesn't meet the criteria for addiction. It's a way for someone to reduce cognitive dissonance about their behavior and how they think of themselves as a person. When it comes to porn, this tendency is especially common with religious men.

A recent study found that people who consider themselves to be very religious have a higher chance of self-identifying as being addicted to internet porn, despite, in some cases, *having only watched it once*[10].

I've seen this sort of thing first-hand with religious men. They'll confess to having an addiction to porn, but when you suss out the extent of the problem, you find out they masturbate to porn two or three times a week. I'm sure for them, their use feels like an addiction (because they don't want to do it at all), but it doesn't come close to being an addiction under the DSM's, or any reasonable, definition.

For these religious men, to view porn is a spiritual transgression and complete abstinence from porn is the ideal. Thus if they find themselves surfing to a porn site once or twice a week to masturbate, there's a dissonance between their behavior and the standard their faith has established. To ease that dissonance, instead of taking responsibility for the spiritual lapse, they pathologize it by calling it an addiction. By so doing they shift their locus of control to an external one and decide that they aren't themselves doing it — instead, porn is doing something to them.

As the researchers of the aforementioned study noted, this *perceived* addiction "has been linked to several real elements of psychological distress, such as depression, compulsive behavior and anxiety." This shouldn't come as a surprise, because remember, that's what happens when you have an external locus of control. Moreover, I'd argue that by calling themselves addicts — even though from a clinical sense they obviously aren't — these men are just making it more difficult to stop looking at porn because the addiction label puts them in a position of helplessness or, worse, they may be creating a self-fulfilling prophecy in which they do become full-blown porn addicts.

So if you're a religious man who happens to use porn a few times a week, don't be so quick to call it an addiction. Sure, it *feels* that way, but calling it such is more likely to hurt than help.

If you're trying to stop using porn (for whatever reason) and you are calling it an addiction, you handicap yourself by starting off with a frame of reference that you don't have, or can't regain, control of your behavior. While acknowledging that porn is a significant problem in your life is healthy, I think there's a point where dialing up the seriousness actually makes it harder to quit. It makes the problem seem like a giant boogeyman, something you won't be able to shake without a big-time intervention, rehab, special expensive retreats, that sort of thing.

If, on the other hand, you think of your porn habit just like any other habit you want to break, that debilitating weight goes away. Telling yourself that you're "changing a habit" seems more in the realm of possibility and puts you in a proactive mindset. Even the way most "porn addiction" experts treat compulsive porn use is exactly the same as how you break any bad habit from swearing to biting your nails; so if you're going to ultimately address the problem as a habit, why not frame it as a habit from the get-go?

For these reasons I think the very best way to frame porn is as "sexual junk food." The all-powerful drive for both food and sex have been around since the dawn of man. We're evolved to eat natural food, intermittently, but now find ourselves with crap-tastic offerings available on every street corner, at every hour of the day. This never-ending glut of junk food can be difficult to resist, but if we don't, we end up obese, anxious, and depressed. In exactly the same way, we're evolved for sex…with flesh and blood humans. But in our modern world, we've got virtual sex on tap 24/7. Gorging ourselves on it diminishes our spirit, enervates our virility, and harms our relationships — all the very best things in life. Porn is sexual junk food that promises nourishment, but leaves us feeling sicker and emptier than before.

In saying using porn is a problem, I've ticked off those who are more liberal on this practice. And now, in saying it should be thought of as a habit rather than an addiction, I've likely earned the ire of those who hold more conservative positions. That's okay with me. I can't stress enough that the reason I think we should frame porn use, even of the compulsive variety, as a habit rather than an addiction is not because I don't think it can be a serious, soul-sucking issue for some men. Rather, I've taken this stance because I know how debilitating a serious porn habit can be. If I thought that labeling compulsive porn use as an addiction could help guys quit, that's how I'd label it. But I earnestly believe that it is quite the opposite.

But What About Porn in Moderation?

At this point, some of you are probably thinking, "But Brett, aren't you making the argument that porn is okay to use in moderation then, if you don't have moral beliefs against it? Does every guy who looks at porn suffer the problems outlined above? If porn is like sexual junk food, isn't it okay to have a Twinkie now and again?"

While I know many would like me to answer these questions with "No way!" that would be disingenuous. Are there some guys out there who use porn in moderation, who don't feel like it's brought serious ill effects into their life, and who don't feel addicted or even compelled to look at it? Sure, definitely. The effects of porn use I have laid out will still exert an influence, but in a much milder way that may not *significantly* interfere with their quality of life.

To return to the junk food analogy, while there are definitely those who can eat one Dorito and stop there, many find stopping at that one chip to be pretty difficult. Knowing this dynamic, there are various courses people choose to take. Some continue their moderate consumption habits, as they enjoy these occasional indulgences and feel confident they can keep them in check. Some have realized they can't just eat one Oreo, and go cold turkey, and thus don't keep it in the house as a temptation. Some are confident they can consume junk food in moderation, but still decide not to touch it, simply because they know it offers little benefit beyond the initial pleasure of ingestion and they enjoy the confidence and health boosts that accompany eating completely "clean."

If you don't have moral compunctions about porn, which course should you take? Can porn be just like eating and drinking alcohol? You will have to weigh what you feel are the pros and cons of porn use for yourself. As you do so, keep in mind the ways that porn consumption is different than that of food or alcohol (or other potentially "addictive" behaviors like video games or exercise):

- Porn is related to our sex drive, and the drive for sexual rewards sits at the very top of the behavior reinforcement hierarchy. So achieving moderation in porn is even harder than it is for something like eating junk food.
- We all need to eat, and even junk food offers calories; you could technically live on Twinkies alone (and a multivitamin). But you can cut out porn from your life altogether.
- Things like food and alcohol have a set satiation and novelty pinnacle — if you develop a tolerance for these substances, you can reach a point where there's

no way to increase the hit you get it. If you develop a tolerance for drinking lighter drinks, you can move to hard liquor, but there's always going to be a point where you black out. (You might move on to harder drugs, then, but you've reached the peak of what alcohol can do for you.) With food, you can't go higher than stuff specifically designed to hit your bliss point. You can eat *more* of it, but once you've tasted all the grocery store's chips and cakes, you've made all the rounds. But with porn, there is an almost infinite variety and endless choices out there. The endless novelty of online porn creates a hungry, hungry itch that may make moderation usage harder to maintain than that of alcohol and food.

- While things like food and alcohol are readily available, nothing matches the availability of porn. You can't press a button and have a Twinkie or a beer appear in your hand, but you can instantly access porn anywhere, anytime from your phone.

- After you eat a Twinkie, you can exercise off the calories, so that it's almost like you never consumed it at all. But the images of porn stay in your head, usually forever.

- Partaking in food and alcohol is a tangible, sensory experience, while porn is almost entirely virtual. While this is not scientifically proven, I feel that increasing levels of abstraction in our life, even in small ways, decreases our sense of well-being. It makes us feel more disconnected from the rhythms of life.

- While food and alcohol can be binged on in private, they also have an important social component. Eating and drinking in moderation can have the benefit of enhancing our relationships, and thus happiness. Viewing porn, though it may be done with one's partner, is almost never done amongst friends, and is most likely to be done alone. It at best does nothing for our sociality, and at worst increases feelings of isolation.

All of which is to say, that compared with other potentially addictive behaviors like eating junk food and drinking alcohol, porn use may be harder to keep in moderation, offers the least benefits, is easiest to cut out of your life completely, and will be missed the least if you do. Its absence may even improve your life. I truly believe it will.

Here's a parallel example from my own life. I used to surf sites like Business Insider and Reddit. I was never addicted to doing so, and this habit never significantly impacted my life in a negative way. But the only pleasure I got from it was brief and mindless, it was an unwelcome distraction from work, and I simply found I felt emptier rather than fuller after doing so. Plus, it was still an itch I had to swat away when I really did need to focus, and every time you resist an impulse you lose a bit of your valuable, limited supply of willpower. So I blocked these sites completely from my computer. My life has not become dramatically different after doing so, but I do feel a little happier and more focused. I could have kept my surfing habit in moderation, but why bother when the modest benefits of cutting it out completely outweigh the inferior "pleasure" I now do without.

When Tim Ferriss (who, from what I can tell, is not a religious guy) cut out porn and masturbation (and booze) for 30 days, he found incredible benefits in doing so, including higher testosterone, greater focus and willpower, and a huge surge in productivity. He was amazed at how "dramatically your life can change if you quit porn and masturbation for a short period."

Bottom line: the less junk you consume in your life — whether that's porn, fast food, or mindless internet surfing — the better and sharper you're going to feel. Yet many men understandably feel that without at least a few "vices," life just ain't worth living. As you mature and decide what indulgences you'd like to keep, and which you'd like to jettison, simply keep in mind the points above; my advice would be to remember that sex is the most powerful drive there is, so if you're going to cut out the junk in any area, that's the category that will give you the most bang for the buck — the most increase in willpower, focus, well-being, and health in your relationships.

If you're not sure how to proceed, why not do an experiment like Ferriss' where you go without porn for a month? If you feel like your life improved, well, you found something that improved your life. If not, well, no harm, no foul. And if you found you couldn't go a whole month without porn, it's time to reevaluate how casual your relationship to porn really is.

If you do decide to quit porn completely, whether for moral or religious reasons or simply because you don't feel it contributes to the excellence of your life, the next chapter offers tips for how to do so.

CHAPTER 3

How to Quit Porn

If you're reading this, you or someone you know is trying to quit porn and is looking for some help in doing so. Here's the good news: in the vast majority of cases, you don't need expensive rehabs or retreats to rid your life of porn. As I mentioned in the last chapter, in reading a boatload of books and countless blog and forum postings on "porn addiction recovery," I discovered that most of the advice given is the exact same advice therapists and cognitive psychologists offer to someone who's trying to change a bad habit as innocuous as swearing or fingernail biting. Sure, there are a few differences, but overall, quitting porn is just like quitting pretty much any other bad habit.

An important thing to keep in mind with changing any habit — be it smoking, drinking soda, or using porn — is that there's no magic bullet. Habit change takes time, discipline, and dedication, and the process will look a little different for each individual.

Progress isn't linear, either. Some weeks you'll feel like you're well on your way to kicking the bad habit and replacing it with a new one, and others you'll have setbacks that will make you feel like crap. That's normal. The key is to not wallow in your setback, but to dust yourself off, and get back in the saddle.

So if you're looking for that one thing that will solve all your problems, you won't find it here. Most of the tips and suggestions that follow are likely things you already know. The only "secret" to habit implementation is having the will to follow through with your intentions. Experiment with the tips in this chapter, and find what works and doesn't work for you.

A Quick Note on Willpower

Before we get into the nitty gritty, let's take a quick look at willpower — both what it is, and how to conserve and strengthen it. Boiled down, willpower is a mental energy that allows you to direct your action. Whenever you have a desire to do something that conflicts with your long-term goals or your core values, willpower is the thing that kicks in and tries to keep you on track. The stronger your willpower is, the better chance of making a decision in line with your goals. It is what allows you to choose your path and to persevere in that path despite obstacles, resistance, and weakness.

It is also helpful to think of your willpower like a muscle. All of these qualities of your muscles also apply to your willpower:

- Your muscles become weak and flabby through disuse and a lack of exercise.
- In order to build the strength of your muscles in the long-term, you must exhaust them in the short-term.
- While you can build the strength of your muscles over time, on any given day when you walk into the gym, your muscles have a finite amount of strength–there's an absolute max weight you can lift before your muscles reach failure.
- If you exhaust your muscles with one exercise, you'll have less strength and endurance on the next exercise because your muscles will be fatigued.

Your muscles need time to recover before they can be fresh again for your next workout.

That's right — willpower is a finite resource that gets exhausted the more you use it. The two things that use it most are exercising self-control (which you may not realize, but happens hundreds of times throughout the day), and simply making decisions, be they small ones like what to have for dinner or big ones like whether to make a big purchase or pursue a new career. If your willpower is depleted at the end of the day, you'll have a harder time saying no to porn. Like anything though, your willpower can be mastered through practice.

To maximize your willpower while quitting porn, make it the primary goal your working towards. While better fitness and healthier eating are obviously worthy pursuits, working on a single goal at a time conserves your willpower to better fight your porn habit. It's also beneficial to create routines for yourself and stick to them. If you have a set morning/evening routine that doesn't include porn, you won't have to wrestle with the decision of whether or not to look at porn. For instance, at night you can simply say you're going to pick up the house for 10 minutes, brush your teeth, journal for 10-15 minutes, and turn the lights out. There's no room for decision making in that process, thereby conserving your willpower.

Reboot and Rewire

Before we get into the specific tips and strategies for quitting porn, it's important to know the two basic parts of the process in your brain: rebooting and rewiring.

REBOOTING

The brain responds to the onslaught of dopamine that comes with constant and escalating porn use by reducing its number of dopamine receptors. This blunting of dopamine sensitivity may lead to problems like erectile dysfunction, delayed ejaculation, depression, and social anxiety.

"Rebooting" refers to taking a break from all artificial sexual stimuli so that the brain can restore and replenish dopamine receptors that were lost in response to the over-consumption of pornography. As Gary Wilson notes in *Your Brain on Porn*, rebooting is a metaphor taken from the computer world: "By avoiding artificial sexual stimulation you are shutting down and restarting the brain, restoring it to its original factory settings." The goal of rebooting is to redis-cover what your life was like before porn.

According to men who have quit and Wilson's observa-tions while working with these men, it may take weeks or months before you begin to see an improvement in porn-related problems. Wilson has noted two patterns of rebooting recovery: One group of men will take just 2-3 weeks before they start seeing improvements to porn-induced ED and the like. The other group, which he calls "long-rebooters," can take 2-6 months to fully recover. The men comprising this group usually started using internet porn at a young age and have been using it for a while. During their brain resets, some long-rebooters report experiencing what they call a "flatline" in which they lose any and all interest in sex for a period of time. However, once the flatline passes, their drive for natural sexual stimulation comes roaring back.

The big rule on rebooting is that you abstain from all *artificial* sexual stimulation. Pornography is the obvious one to abstain from, but veteran rebooters recommend also nixing things like "erotic literature," sexy YouTube videos, Victoria's Secret catalogs, etc. Fantasies about porn should also be avoided (which I imagine is easier said than done).

While *artificial* sexual stimulation must be avoided during the reboot phase, natural sexual stimulation like actual sex is fine. Some say sexual fantasies (about real life sex) and masturbation are okay too, but of course others will have religious compunctions against these practices. While natural sexual stimulation is a-okay, some reboot veterans recommend taking a break from *all* sex and masturbation for a bit to help speed along the process. Each man is different in his needs and beliefs, so experimenting is key.

If you've experienced some of the problems that are associated with heavy porn use, then the reboot phase is a necessary first step for you, and our tips below will help you in your quest to go porn-free.

If you haven't had any porn-related problems, then you might not notice drastic changes in yourself except for the fact that you're no longer using porn.

Finally, if you don't see any improvements after a prolonged reboot, you need to be open to the possibility that there's some underlying problem with your sexual, erectile health that's not related to porn, and you may need additional help treating it.

REWIRING

If you feel like you can't stop looking at porn, that's because you've likely created a very strong habit in the reward circuitry of your brain. Your internet porn use has rewired your neurons so that whenever you encounter an external or internal cue associated with porn, you go into auto-pilot mode and begin the routine of searching for it. For example, sitting down at your computer when no one else is around can serve as a cue that leads you almost automatically to clicking on your porn files.

The goal of the rewiring phase is to replace the routine of looking at porn when you encounter a cue for it, with something that's *not* looking at internet porn. For example, you have a journal that sits next to your computer, and whenever you sit down, the first thing you do is write a few sentences in it. We're replacing a bad habit with a good habit.

One thing to keep in mind with habit change and "rewiring": neuroscientists have learned that once our brain encodes a habit, it never really disappears. It's always there looking for that certain cue to initiate the habit sequence.

The permanence of bad habits shouldn't discourage you; change is still possible according to the latest habit research. While you can't completely get rid of a bad habit, it is possible to create more powerful good habits that simply override the bad ones. That's what rewiring is all about.

The tips below will help you stay away from porn, even when the itch remains strong during the reboot phase, as well as help you rewire your brain so your no-porn habit sticks.

Tips on How to Successfully Reboot, Rewire, and Quit Porn for Good

Alright, let's get into the nitty gritty of how to actually quit using porn for good. The tips and suggestions below are based on my research into cognitive psychology over the years as well as from reported experiences of men who have quit using porn. Again, there's no silver bullet. What works for one man, may not work for you. You need to be ready to experiment and try different things.

The advice below can be broken into two parts: mindset and action.

MINDSET

1. Don't Give Porn More Power Than It Should Have

"When you characterize porn as an addiction it tells you that it is hard to break free, that it is a struggle, that relapse is inevitable — all things that have nothing to do with porn. But when you characterize online porn as junk food, the solution is obvious: don't eat it."

– The Last Psychiatrist

Among men who are trying to quit, it's popular to conjure up images of porn being an unbeatable dark monster/plague/pandemic/war that must be fought tooth and nail and if you succumb to it, you're destined to becoming a goat rapist, or something. But I don't think that mindset is very helpful. In fact, firebrand rhetoric like that can actually backfire. Research suggests that this sort of simplistic, over-the-top rhetoric was the big reason the D.A.R.E. Program failed to reduce drug use amongst American teenagers back in the 80s and 90s. One study even showed that compared to middle schoolers who didn't take part in the program, D.A.R.E. students showed an *increase* in the use of drugs! D.A.R.E. inadvertently made drugs alluring by giving them the aura of "forbidden fruit," tempting kids who otherwise wouldn't have given drugs much thought.

I think we'd do well to take a lesson from how Superman defeated the KKK in how we should approach porn. Yes, Superman. After WWII, the Ku Klux Klan experienced a resurgence in membership in some parts of the U.S.A. Florida activist and folklorist Stetson Kennedy decided to take on the Klan and began infiltrating meetings in hopes of exposing the Klan's secrets. After Kennedy learned how Klansmen identified each other, he went to the local police with the info in the hopes they could use it to start arresting members of the organization. But the police sat on their hands because they were too afraid of the Klan's power.

So Stetson went to the producers of the mega-popular *Superman* radio program and asked if they'd be interested in creating a "Superman vs. the Klan" plot line for the show. The producers were game and so began a 16-episode series in which Superman took on the Klan. During the episodes, Klan secrets like handshakes, rituals, and passwords were divulged. Almost overnight, KKK recruitment dried up and local authorities started cracking down on Klansmen who were flagrantly and openly violating the law.

Why the change? Part of the power of the KKK was their "air of menace" that came with clouding themselves in a shroud of secrecy. Once Superman revealed their secrets, the group didn't seem all that scary or powerful anymore.

I think we can and should do something similar with porn. One of the most powerful things that can help you quit using porn is simply understanding how it affects your brain and why it's so alluring. Instead of seeming like some mysterious, menacing, unstoppable force, your attraction for porn is revealed as a perfectly natural drive that's been hijacked by a supernormal reproductive and evolutionary reinforcer.

Once you understand the science behind porn use, you can see it for what it really is: sexual junk food. You don't give your bag of potato chips a menacing aura of power. They're just potato chips. If you want to quit eating potato chips, you learn about the different ways carbs vs. protein and veggies affects your body, you throw away your potato chips, you quit going down the potato chip aisle in the grocery store, and you choose the celery stick at the party. Try doing the same thing with internet pornography.

I know some might think that's a flippant comparison, particularly if they've seen porn destroy marriages and relationships, but I think understanding the problem and making it approachable is truly the key to success here. It puts you in a proactive place where you can confidently start taking steps to kick the habit.

There's wisdom in following the advice of the 17th century Jesuit priest Baltasar Gracian: *Undertake what's easy as if it were hard, and what's hard as if it were easy.*

A Note on Shame and the Ineffective Way in Which Porn Is Typically Taught at Church

The folks who are most concerned about porn tend to be religious, and they see porn as a spiritual cancer.

And yet the way that porn is more often than not discussed at church tends to be incredibly counterproductive, driving men deeper into porn use instead of away from it.

If you're a regular reader of AoM, you'll know I've talked about the fact that shame can be an unmatchable motivator for seeking positive improvement. But that's only if it's simultaneously accompanied by both the will to do better and the confidence that you can improve. If shame is just a trigger for self-pity and endless rumination about how you're a terrible person, the effect is exactly the opposite. Excess shame becomes debilitating.

That's why, and this relates to the points made above, I think it's actually highly ineffective to go overboard on demonizing porn use. Yes, for Christian guys, it's a sin, and I've got nothing against calling it such. But porn frequently gets weighted with more baggage than its fellow transgressions; Jesus said simply looking at a woman with lust was adultery, and yet if we catch a young man ogling a woman's cleavage we tend to just smack him in the head and tell him to cut it out. Yet if he looks at a pair of breasts online — whoa-ho-ho! — he is sick! Filthy! Depraved! On the pathway to addiction and Hell! All this overweening smack down accomplishes is leading the porn user to withdraw, to hide his dirty secret at all costs from his friends and family, to suffer crushing guilt and anxiety, and to feel hopelessly defective, which all leads back to…more porn to soothe his feelings of stress and isolation! I truly believe that excess shame is frequently what turns casual porn use into a compulsion.

Demonizing porn also has the unfortunate side effect of seeping over into demonizing sexuality itself, which can give some men a complex about their own natural and healthy sexuality, which can in turn frustrate future sexual relationships (again, leading the man back to porn) and his relationships with women in general. Some men go so overboard with their antipathy towards porn that they can't look at a 1950s pin-up poster without being scandalized, or a scantily-clad woman at church without chastising her for being "living porn" and sabotaging his efforts to keep his mind clean.

If a loved one or someone at your church is having a problem with porn, it's okay to express disappointment, and it's okay for the man to feel some healthy shame for the way in which he's fallen short of your shared ideals. But don't heap on the scorn. Teach young men that sexuality is a healthy, wonderful thing. Teach them that their attraction to porn is a very normal consequence of their biology and brains, that they should try not to slip up, but if they do, to just get right back in the saddle and keep on trucking.

2. **Accept the Fact That You're the Kind of Guy Who Looks at Porn (And Understand That the Goal is to Become the Kind of Guy Who Doesn't Look at Porn)**

Aristotle said, "We are what we repeatedly do." And it's true. Cognitive psychology has shown again and again that our behavior shapes how we think and feel. Action shapes who we are.

If you look at porn on a regular basis, you need to accept the fact that you're the kind of guy who looks at porn.

That might be a hard pill to swallow, especially if porn viewing goes against your religious beliefs. But pathologizing away the fact by calling your porn viewing an addiction just makes the problem harder to overcome because you're giving yourself an external locus of control.

Acceptance doesn't mean resignation. You're not doomed to being "that guy who looks at porn" for the rest of your life. It just means you see the situation for what it is so you can start making proactive changes.

Instead of trying to "beat" the "addiction," a more helpful goal is to simply become the kind of guy who doesn't look at porn. I know. Easier said than done. But think about it this way: if you see yourself as a guy who has to try really, really hard not to look at porn, instead of as a guy who just doesn't look at porn because he's got other interests, you're in for a real slog through life.

The way you get to be the "guy who doesn't look at porn" is to start acting like a guy who doesn't look at porn. Act as if; fake it until you make it. I'm not saying this approach will make things easy, particularly in the beginning of trying to quit, but it can help make quitting porn feel like less of a battle and more of an effort to change for the better.

3. Address Underlying Issues

Sometimes guys get depressed because they use porn, and sometimes they use porn because they're depressed. If it's the latter case for you, simply quitting porn is not going to solve all your problems. So an important first step in quitting porn is to address any underlying issues you have going on. Are you simply bored? Get involved in more hobbies, social activities, and working out. You'll be amazed at how simply having a fun, full, busy life will take away your need for porn and masturbation. Has your sex life died down with your significant other? Talk to her about your needs.

It can be tempting to think that the changing of life's circumstances will be the thing that finally helps you quit. "Once I graduate and I'm a real man, then I'll be done with porn." "Once I have a regular sex life, then I'll be done with porn." "Once I get married and start a family, then I'll be done with porn." While it can be true for some guys that all they need is a single life trigger like this, expecting it to happen that way will only delay your addressing these underlying issues. If you find yourself coming up with these types of excuses, know that there's likely something else that needs to be changed in your life that you are in control of, even if it just comes down to boredom.

4. Believe You Can Change

Yes, you can change. Research shows that even the most ingrained habits or traits can be modified and improved upon. But you have to believe you can change.

Charles Duhigg, author of *The Power of Habit*, points out that research suggests that the people who have the most success in changing bad habits simply believe that change is possible. The importance of belief in changing habits may explain the correlation between religious belief and how long a person stays sober when trying to quit alcohol. A study found that alcoholics who had a belief in a higher power were more likely to stay on the wagon even during stressful moments than alcoholics who didn't have that belief.

So if you're a religious guy, embrace your faith. Say your prayers, fast, read your scriptures. Along with some of the techniques provided below, they can help turn not watching porn into a permanent behavior change.

But what if you're not religious? Well, here's the thing: these same researchers found that believing in a higher power, like God, wasn't necessary. You just had to have the capacity to believe that things can get better. Being part of a group of other people who have changed a bad habit can help spur belief. You can look around the room or forum and think, "If it worked for that guy, maybe it can work for me."

Change is possible. You're not stuck with your bad habits, but you have to believe it in order for it to fully work.

5. Don't Beat Yourself Up If and When You Backslide

Your emotions can serve as a cue to start looking at porn. Many guys will pull up a browser when they're depressed or feel down as a way to self-soothe. But the problem that many men who are trying to quit porn run into is that their setbacks make them feel down or depressed, which in turn triggers the itch to look at porn again. It's a vicious cycle.

What's more, as we noted previously, intense emotions like shame and guilt can also cause spikes in dopamine. So if you experience a lot of guilt and shame after a setback, you may be making the porn habit worse.

Just accept the fact that you may have setbacks. Maybe you won't, but most men who are trying to quit do. When those setbacks happen, don't beat yourself up or wallow in self-pity. Just recognize the setback and then get back at it again. You may even consider "parenting" yourself by setting up some sort of swift, dispassionate "punishment" for your slip-ups, like donating a few bucks to a charity you dislike, or to the political party opposite of yours. The key is to be consistent and dispassionate with your negative feedback.

6.   Find Ways to Conserve and Strengthen Willpower

A big part of kicking the porn habit is resisting those impulses to watch porn when you encounter one of your behavioral cues. That takes willpower. Read our series on how to conserve and strengthen your willpower so you can say no to the itch to itch your wiener: artofmanliness.com/tag/willpower.

The cool thing is that by quitting porn, you'll strengthen your overall willpower supply, so you'll have more of this potent power to use on all the other goals in your life.

7. Strengthen Your Resilience

One thing the can help you handle setbacks and shift from an external to an internal locus of control is working on building your resilience. We did a whole series on it a few years ago that you can access for free on the site: artofmanliness.com/tag/resiliency. If you'd like all the content in one place, check out our ebook version, available at store.artofmanliness.com.

ACTIONS

8. Get Rid of All Your Porn

Start off with a clean slate by going through your house and computer and clearing out any porn you have. Clear out your computer's and smartphone's web history, cache, and bookmarks. If you have magazines and DVDs, throw those out too.

9. Hack the Habit Loop

This is probably the most important tip, so pay special attention. The rewiring process is essentially the same as hacking the habit loop, which Charles Duhigg covered in *The Power of Habit*, and which we've written before on artofmanliness.com. Your goal is to identify the cues that trigger your porn surfing routine and then to substitute that routine with something else while keeping the reward the same (or similar). Each time you do that you're creating a new reward connection that can eventually become stronger than your porn routine connection.

With porn use, the reward your brain is craving is dopamine, so the most effective way to hack your habit loop is to replace it with something that gives you that hit. Here are some activities that produce dopamine:

- Eat a carby snack
- Exercise
- Play video games
- Take a nap
- Work on a goal
- Call a friend who can make you laugh

Obviously, some of these rewards aren't strictly healthy either, but they may constitute the lesser of two evils in your life.

Here's an example of how hacking the habit loop works. If one of your internal cues to look at porn is feeling bored, decide that whenever a bout of boredom hits, instead of getting on the computer, where your search for porn will assuredly begin, you practice your guitar.

10. Have Implementation Intentions at the Ready

An important part of hacking the habit loop is establishing implementation intentions. In a nutshell, an implementation intention is an "if-then" phrase that links a situational cue to a specific action. It's a plan of what you're going to do differently whenever you encounter one of your porn cues.

So if one of your cues is feeling depressed, an implementation intention would look something like: *When I feel depressed, I will go outside and take a walk.*

You may need multiple implementation intentions if you have multiple cues. It's also a good idea to have a plan for what you're going to do when you randomly stumble upon porn or a provocative image that sets off a trigger. It could be something as drastic as shutting down the computer or something as simple as immediately closing your browser. Or if you come across something on TV, you get up and leave.

Jumping up from your chair at the sight of porn may make you feel rather silly, and contradict your image of yourself as cool and rational, but it's just a way of dislodging your brain from following the well-worn groove that porn has carved out in your neurons. You've got to shake those neurons up. Don't let feeling cool and calm get in the way of improving your life.

11. Install Blocking Software on All Your Digital Devices

Many men find putting blocking software on their devices helpful, especially in the early stages of rebooting when willpower to check porn is weakest and the habit to do it is strongest. However, it should be noted that blocking software isn't fail-proof and is easy to get around. Its main benefit is to put up a barrier or speed bump between the cue to look at porn and you actually scratching that itch. Hopefully as you start going through settings and entering in passwords to remove the block, you'll catch yourself and begin using one of your implementation intentions.

Here are a few suggestions on how to block porn sites that you visit frequently:

a. Use Your Computer's Parental Controls

Create a separate account on your computer for your work and then use the admin account to set up parental controls that block certain sites on the web. That speed bump might be enough for you to stop looking at porn when you get the urge. However, if you feel like you need to, have a friend create a new password for your admin account and not tell you what it is.

b. Change Your Host Files

Updating your host files on your computer simply means telling your device that your favorite porn sites live on your computer's hard drive. Because these websites don't *really* live on your hard drive, you'll get a "server not found" message when you try to surf to those addresses. Doesn't matter what browser you're on. I've had great success with this method to help me stop visiting time-wasting websites like HuffPo. I've had them blocked in my host files for years. In the beginning, I kept checking back to those sites out of habit, but eventually I stopped, and now I don't even have the itch to visit them any more.

While this method is reversible, it's kind of a pain in the butt to change. Any time you want to visit your blocked sites, you'll have to go through the rigmarole below and "comment out" your added lines (add a # to the beginning of the lines) in your host file.

Here's how it works, using Facebook.com as an example:

Mac

1. Open up Terminal (find it using the Spotlight tool)

2. Type sudo nano /etc/hosts

3. Enter your computer's password

4. To block your time-wasting sites, type in the following: 127.0.0.1   facebook.com

5. Repeat step 4 until you've entered all your time-wasting sites

6. Save the host file by hitting ctrl+o and then the return key

7. Flush your computer's cache by entering the following line: sudo dscacheutil -flushcache

Windows (Windows 8/7/Vista/XP)

1. Open Notepad and click File –> Open

2. Open up the following file: C:\WINDOWS\SYSTEM32\DRIVERS\ETC\HOSTS

3. To block your time-wasting sites, type in the following: 127.0.0.1 facebook.com www.facebook.com

4. Repeat step 3 until you've entered all your time-wasting sites

5. Save the file and close

Linux

If you're using Linux, you're probably a geek and don't need some guy who blogs about manliness to tell you how to edit your host file.

c. Web Filters

Web filters can be installed on your computer or even wireless router so that porn sites are blocked when you try to visit them. There are several free options that work well.

OpenDNS. It's free. Just install it on your wireless router and select the level of filtering you want. Anytime you try to visit a site that's been categorized as "pornographic," you'll get a message that says, "This domain is blocked." Setting up can be tricky. For some reason, OpenDNS only works intermittently on my Chrome browser. Just tried visiting playboy.com and was able to get through on Chrome, but it's blocked in Safari.

K9 Protection. Another popular free filter. Though many guys report that it's not all that helpful unless you give the password to somebody else so you're not tempted to turn it off. Another trick could be coming up with such a long and random string of characters (we're talking 50+ here) that the hassle of entering in the password keeps you from turning it off.

Net Nanny. Net Nanny is a paid web filtering service that's pretty robust. It can block access to pornographic sites not just on your computer, but also your wirelessly connected devices.

Self Control for Mac. It's a free open-source Mac app that allows you to block sites for a pre-determined amount of time (or indefinitely). Until the timer expires, you'll be unable to access those sites — even if you restart your computer or delete the app.

Cold Turkey. A similar app for Windows. It's pretty robust and could even be used to block time-wasting sites.

d. Blocking Sites On Mobile Devices

Parental Controls

Just use your smartphone's or mobile device's parental controls to block the sites that give you trouble. If you need to, have a friend change your password so you can't change it for a while.

How to Block Sites on Your Apple Devices
http://aom.is/o3V6o

How to Block Sites on Your Android Devices
There are number of parental control apps in the Google Play Store that will allow you to block certain sites.

Parental Control. Allows you to block certain sites, features, and apps on your phone or tablet for certain periods of time.

Self Control. This app will allow you to block certain apps for a certain period of time (or indefinitely). You might consider blocking access to your browser.

12. Don't Go It Alone: Get an Accountability Partner

A common tactic to beating any habit is getting an accountability partner — someone you report to when you have a slip-up. Accountability partners add a small sting of healthy social shame so that you're persuaded not to look at porn because you don't want to fess up to it. They're also there to offer support and encouragement so that you get back into the saddle.

Pick someone you trust and have a strong relationship with. Could be a brother or a friend. Each day, or each week, just let him know how you did. It can be an embarrassing topic to bring up in the first place, so you'll have to courage-up and know that thousands of other men are dealing with the same struggle.

If you can't trust yourself to self-disclose, consider installing accountability software on your computer that sends an email to a close friend or confidant whenever you visit a questionable site. The specter of being watched can keep you from visiting your favorite porn sites.

X3 Watch. There are both free and premium versions. Works across devices and operating systems. With the free version, you can pick up to two accountability partners. Each week they'll get an email report of the questionable sites you've visited. If you upgrade to the premium version, they'll get instant notifications. Just FYI: this software is associated with xxxchurch.com, a Christian ministry that's dedicated to fighting porn.

CovenantEyes. Similar service to X3. Again, for those who care, CovenantEyes has a Christian angle to it.

Join a Forum. Other men who have successfully kicked the porn habit have credited the myriad of forums on the web that are dedicated to helping men stop using porn. They swap stories on the problems porn have caused, what they did to kick the habit, and the positives that have come from quitting porn. They also find support for those times they backslide.

r/NoFap. It's a Reddit subreddit and is the largest quitting porn forum on the web. These 123K "fapstronauts" ("fap" is slang for masturbating) track their progress with not masturbating to porn (or without it) and offer support for others who want to do the same.

r/pornfree. Similar to NoFap but with a focus on breaking the porn habit.

Reboot Nation. Started and operated by a guy named Gabe who suffered from porn-induced ED and cured it after he eliminated porn from his life. Men who want to stop porn can start journals in the forum to track their progress and get advice and support from other members. Gabe also has lots of resources on the forum about the effects of porn.

Your Brain Rebalanced. Another place where people trying to quit porn can start a journal to track their progress and get support from other members. They break down journals by age groups so you can see what porn-induced problems men your age might face and what they did to overcome them.

At a certain point in your progress, it may be useful to stop visiting these forums because they simply serve as a reminder of pornography. (Don't think of a pink elephant!) Remember, the ultimate goal is to become the kind of person who simply doesn't look at porn. Visiting these sites may reinforce your self-identity as a guy who has to try really, really hard not to look at porn.

13. Track Progress (Or Not)

Much like alcoholics do, many self-described porn addicts track the number of days since they last used porn. Being able to see how far you've progressed can certainly act as motivation to keep chugging on. Apps like HabitForge, Chain Calendar, or Joe's Goals are great ways to track your progress of being porn free.

But like visiting quitting porn forums, there may come a moment in your progress when you'll want to quit tracking because it's no longer useful and continues to reinforce the idea that you're a guy who looks at porn, but has to try really hard not to.

Studies show that "gamifying" habit change can help with motivation. An anti-porn organization called Fight the New Drug have developed an online program called Fortify that has video courses, tracking, and game-like aspects to help you quit porn for good.

14. Fast and Exercise

If you're experiencing problems linked to dulled dopamine sensitivity due to overconsumption of porn, research suggests that fasting and exercise can help replenish them. In a study on obese rats, researchers found that dopamine receptors increased when the rats intermittently fasted or went without food for a period of time. It might not hurt to give intermittent fasting a try to help your reboot along. On top of possibly replenishing damaged dopamine receptors, fasting is an exercise in willpower, which can help strengthen your willpower to say no to porn. A simple way to implement intermittent fasting is to begin your fast at 7 or 8 PM and then skip breakfast and don't eat until lunch. From 12PM until 7PM you can eat.

Strenuous anaerobic exercise has also been shown to have a strengthening effect on dopamine receptors. Strenuous anaerobic exercise would be things like lifting heavy weights or doing HIIT or CrossFit. If you're not already, start adding exercise into your routine to help with your effort to reboot. Exercise is also a fantastic release of boredom, tension, and stress – if you sweat out these emotions at the gym, you'll likely feel less need to do so through porn and masturbation.

Conclusion

I hope you found this book on the science of pornography useful or at least interesting. For those of you who have been wanting to kick the porn habit but have had trouble, I hope we provided some new insights on why it's been a struggle; understanding why porn is so alluring and why you have the habit in the first place can go a long way in removing some of the psychological power that porn has over you. If you're looking for more information on porn's effect on the brain, I highly recommend going over to Gary Wilson's site, YourBrainOnPorn.com or picking up his ebook. Wilson's is by far the best book on porn I read during the course of the research; there's no religious slant or over-the-top rhetoric. Just helpful information.

If you don't think porn is wrong, and don't personally have a problem with it, I hope you still found this information interesting. Our culture's view of porn tends to be one-dimensional and it's always a good exercise to look at the other side of things. Just as we try to educate folks about the possible drawbacks of other vices like alcohol or tobacco so that they can make better, more informed choices about their use of those products, we should start doing so with pornography. Even if you don't have a problem with porn, you might know someone who does, and it's good for parents to openly talk to their kids about it so it's not something they mind-lessly fall into.

At the end of the day, that should really be the goal for all of us: to approach the use of porn in our lives as mindfully as possible.

Resources to Help You Overcome Porn Use

Throughout the book I mentioned several resources to help you overcome porn. I thought it would be helpful to have them all in one place.

BOOKS

Your Brain on Porn: Internet Pornography and the Emerging Science of Addiction by **Gary Wilson.** The best book about the science of porn's effect on your brain. I highly recommend you pick up a copy. It's only available on Amazon Kindle.

Wired for Intimacy: How Pornography Hijacks the Male Brain by **William M. Struthers.** While this book takes a Christian approach to pornography, the author, William Struthers, is a professor of psychology and spends a great deal of time explaining what happens in your brain whenever you view porn. I couldn't find a better explanation of all the neural processes that take place any where else.

The Power of Habit by **Charles Duhigg.** The best book on how to change even the most engrained of habits.

WEBSITES

YourBrainOnPorn.com. Website run by Gary Wilson that's packed with information about the ill effects of over consuming internet porn.

Reboot Nation. Started and operated by a guy named Gabe who suffered from porn-induced ED and cured it after he eliminated porn from his life. Men who want to stop porn can start journals in the forum to track their progress and get advice and support from other members. Gabe also has lots of resources on the forum about the effects of porn.

Your Brain Rebalanced. Another place where people trying to quit porn can start a journal to track their progress and get support from other members. They break down journals by age groups so you can see what porn-induced problems men your age might face and what they did to overcome them.

Fight the New Drug. A non-profit organization dedicated to educating about the ill-effects of porn use as well as helping individuals overcome their porn habit. Lots of great content and research posted their regularly.

r/noFap. It's a Reddit subreddit and is the largest quitting porn forum on the web. These 123K "fapstronauts" ("fap" is slang for masturbating) track their progress with not masturbating to porn (or without it) and offer support for others who want to do the same.

r/pornfree. Similar to NoFap but with a focus on breaking the porn habit.

Web Filters

OpenDNS. It's free. Just install it on your wireless router and select the level of filtering you want. Anytime you try to visit a site that's been categorized as "pornographic," you'll get a message that says, "This domain is blocked." Setting up can be tricky.

K9 Protection. Another popular free filter. Though many guys report that it's not all that helpful unless you give the password to somebody else so you're not tempted to turn it off. Another trick could be coming up with such a long and random string of characters (we're talking 50+ here) that the hassle of entering in the password keeps you from turning it off.

Net Nanny. Net Nanny is a paid web filtering service that's pretty robust. It can block access to pornographic sites not just on your computer, but also your wirelessly connected devices.

Self Control for Mac. It's a free open-source Mac app that allows you to block sites for a pre-determined amount of time (or indefinitely). Until the timer expires, you'll be unable to access those sites — even if you restart your computer or delete the app.

Cold Turkey for Windows. A similar app for Windows. It's pretty robust and could even be used to block time-wasting sites.

Parental Control. (For Android devices) Allows you to block certain sites, features, and apps on your phone or tablet for certain periods of time.

Self Control. (For Android devices) This app will allow you to block certain apps for a certain period of time (or indefinitely). You might consider blocking access to your browser.

ACCOUNTABILITY PROGRAMS

X3 Watch. There are both free and premium versions. Works across devices and operating systems. With the free version, you can pick up to two accountability partners. Each week they'll get an email report of the questionable sites you've visited. If you upgrade to the premium version, they'll get instant notifications. Just FYI: this software is associated with xxxchurch.com, a Christian ministry that's dedicated to fighting porn.

CovenantEyes. Similar service to X3. Again, for those who care, CovenantEyes has a Christian angle to it.

Habit Trackers

Fortify. An online program that "gamifies" breaking the porn habit with badges, trackers, and video courses.

Pavlok. Pavlok is the first device that changes what we do.

Using vibration, beeps, and even electric shock, Pavlok helps you break bad habits and train your behavior. Unlike other devices, Pavlok can be worn anywhere on your body — not just on your wrist. Pavlok provides instant feedback on when you're doing what you're not supposed to be doing and not doing what you want to be doing

You can use Pavlok's API to make it vibrate or shock you when you try to surf to your favorite porn sites. You can even have Pavlok post to your Facebook profile if you visited a porn site. Talk about a huge disincentive to look at porn!

Chain Calendar. Inspired by a productivity and goal achieving secret from Jerry Seinfeld, the Chain Calendar is a free, portable web tool so you can track your goals online. Track the days you go porn-free and try not to break that chain!

Joe's Goals. Free online habit tracker.

Habit RPG. Turn breaking a habit into a game with Habit RPG. It's pretty cool. If you're a fan of RPG games like Dungeons and Dragons for Final Fantasy, you'll love this app.

ENDNOTES

Introduction

1. Hewlett, Barry S., and Bonnie L. Hewlett. "Sex and Searching For Children Among Aka Foragers and Ngandu Farmers of Central America." African Study Monographs 31.3 (2010): 107-25. Web. <http://jambo. africa.kyoto-u.ac.jp/kiroku/asm_normal/abstracts/pdf/31-3/107-125.pdf>.

Chapter 1: Why is the Pull of Porn So Strong?

1. Sato, Satoru M., Kalynn M. Schulz, Cheryl L. Sisk, and Ruth I. Wood. "Adolescents and Androgens, Receptors and Rewards." Hormones and Behavior 53.5 (2008): 647-58. Web. <http://www.sciencedirect.com/science/article/pii/S0018506X08000305>.

2. Beach, Frank A., and Lisbeth Jordan. "Sexual Exhaustion and Recovery in the Male Rat." Quarterly Journal of Experimental Psychology 8.3 (1956): 121-33. Web. <http://www.tandfonline.com/doi/abs/10.1080/17470215608416811#.VcJdn_nLHIV>.

3. Koukounas, Eric, and Ray Over. "Changes in the Magnitude of the Eyeblink Startle Response during Habituation of Sexual Arousal." Behaviour Research and Therapy 38.6 (2000): 573-84. Web. <http://www.ncbi.nlm.nih.gov/pubmed/10846806>.

4. Nestler, EJ. "Is There a Common Molecular Pathway for Addiction?" Nature Neuroscience 8.11 (2005): 1445-449. Web. <http://www.ncbi.nlm.nih.gov/pubmed/16251986>.

5. Pitchers, K.K. "Natural and Drug Rewards Act on Common Neural Plasticity Mechanisms with ΔFosB

as a Key Mediator." The Journal of Neuroscience 33.8 (2013): 3434-432. Web. <http://www.ncbi.nlm.nih.gov/pubmed/23426671>.

Chapter 2: The Possible Pitfalls of Porn

1. "Italian Men Suffer 'sexual Anorexia' after Internet Porn Use." ANSA.it. N.p., 24 Feb. 2011. Web. <http://www.ansa.it/web/notizie/rubriche/english/2011/02/24/visual-izza_new.html_1583160579.html>.

2. Wosnitzer, Robert, and Ana Bridges. "Aggression and Sexual Behavior in Best-selling Pornography Videos: A Content Analysis Update." Violence Against Women 16.10 (2010): 1065-085. Web. <http://www.ncbi.nlm.nih.gov/pubmed/20980228>.

3. Voon, Valerie. "Neural Correlates of Sexual Cue Reactivity in Individuals with and without Compulsive Sexual Behaviours." PLoS One (2014): n. pag. Web. <http://journals.plos.org/plosone/article?id=10.1371/journal.pone.0102419>.

4. Stewart, Destin N., and Dawn M. Szymanski. "Young Adult Women's Reports of Their Male Romantic Partner's Pornography Use as a Correlate of Their Self-Esteem, Relationship Quality, and Sexual Satisfaction." Sex Roles 67.5-6 (2012): 257-71. Web. <http://link.springer.com/article/10.1007/s11199-012-0164-0>.

5. Weir, Kirsten. "Is Pornography Addictive?" Monitor on Psychology Apr. 2014: 46. APA.org. Web. <http://www.apa.org/monitor/2014/04/pornography.aspx>.

6. Gholipour, Bahar. "Teen Anal Sex Study: 6 Unexpected Findings." Live Science. N.p., 13 Aug. 2014. Web. <http://www.livescience.com/47352-teen-anal-sex-unexpected-findings.html>.

7. "Dopamine May Play New Role in Depression." WebMD. N.p., 28 July 2005. Web. <http://www.webmd.com/depression/news/20050728/dopamine-may-play-new-role-in-depression>.

8. Schneier, Franklin R. "Low Dopamine D2 Receptor Binding Potential in Social Phobia." The American Journal of Psychiatry 157.3 (2000): 457-59. Web. <http://ajp.psychiatryonline.org/doi/abs/10.1176/appi.ajp.157.3.457>.

9. Goldstein, Rita Z., and Nora D. Volkow. "Dysfunction of the Prefrontal Cortex in Addiction: Neuroimaging Findings and Clinical Implications." Nature Reviews Neuroscience 12 (2011): 652-69. Web. <http://www.nature.com/nrn/journal/v12/n11/full/nrn3119.html>.

10. Grubbs, Joshua B. "Transgression as Addiction: Religiosity and Moral Disapproval as Predictors of Perceived Addiction to Pornography." Archives of Sexual Behavior 44.1 (2015): 125-36. Web. <http://link.springer.com/article/10.1007%2Fs10508-013-0257-z#page-1>.

Made in the USA
Middletown, DE
02 July 2019